Space Hero

Annie Broadhead
and Ginni Light

Space Hero

PENGUIN ENGLISH

PENGUIN BOOKS

Published by the Penguin Group
Penguin Books Ltd, 27 Wrights Lane, London W8 5TZ, England
Viking Penguin, a division of Penguin Books USA Inc.
375 Hudson Street, New York, New York 10014, USA
Penguin Books Australia Ltd, Ringwood, Victoria, Australia
Penguin Books Canada Ltd, 2801 John Street, Markham, Ontario, Canada L3R 1B4
Penguin Books (NZ) Ltd, 182–190 Wairau Road, Auckland 10, New Zealand

Penguin Books Ltd, Registered Offices: Harmondsworth, Middlesex, England

First published by Penguin Books 1986
3 5 7 9 10 8 6 4 2

Typeset in 11/14pt Linotron Zapf Book Light

Made and printed in Great Britain by
BPCC Hazell Books
Aylesbury, Bucks, England
Member of BPCC Ltd.

CONTENTS

INTRODUCTION

Adventure Gamebooks allow readers to take part in their own story. At the end of many of the sections readers are asked to make a choice. They then turn to the relevant section to continue their own particular story.

Each book consists of a series of interwoven short stories. Readers will not usually read the whole of each book, but, by making their own choices, will read one of the short stories.

Readers can then go back and make different choices and give their story a different direction. In this way the book can be extended or reused, and the stories become quite different.

1

It is the year 2500. You are the captain of a spaceship. You often travel around the Galaxy, but usually you work at the base station on Earth. You are working with communications systems.

One day, a very strange message comes through the computer. Nobody can understand the message because it is in a strange language. You are an expert on the languages of other planets. When you read the message it says, 'Please help us. We live on Nirius. Our enemy the Platons are coming. They are going to kill us and take our planet.'

This situation is very dangerous. The Platons are also Earth's enemy. They will kill you too, if you help the Nirians. But you must help. You must go. There are two spaceships you can take: the *Colomba*, an old spaceship, or a special Warship with many new weapons. In the *Colomba* everyone will think you are on a routine trip into space. In the Warship, everyone will know you are going to fight someone. Do you take the *Colomba* (turn to **17**) or do you take the Warship (turn to **25**)?

2

This is the most important and the most difficult part of your journey. There are six Platon Warships and you are only one. You must surprise the Platons and attack first. You must act quickly. The missiles are ready. You can fire two at the same time.

You fire them. Two of the Platon Warships explode and disappear into space. There are still four more. You must prepare another two missiles very quickly. You fire another two and hit another two Platon Warships.

Unfortunately the other two Platon Warships are now in a position to fire at you. They fire. One missile hits the side of your Warship.

You fire another two missiles. The last two Platon Warships explode. Great! You have destroyed the Platons. Well done! Now you can land on Nirius. Turn to **69**.

3

You can see the storm on your monitor. You change the direction of the *Colomba*. You are now travelling towards an area called 'Paradise'. Not many people from Earth have been there before. But one man who went there and came back called it 'Paradise' because it is so beautiful. There are many small green planets. The climate is wonderful, and there are gardens, lakes and forests. Nobody has ever seen the people who live there.

Last year a spaceship from Earth, with six men on board, went into this area and it never came back. They sent no message back to Earth. There are many stories about this. Some people say that the Earthmen are now living a wonderful life on one of these planets and that they do not want to come back to Earth.

One of your crew, John, is very interested in these stories. He says to you, 'We are passing very close to one of these planets. Could we land on it, just for an hour? We are already twelve hours late. Another hour won't make any difference.'

You are quite interested too, but you know it is important to get to Nirius. Do you land on the green planet (turn to **71**) or do you continue to Nirius (turn to **56**)?

4

You decide to land on the nearest planet. It is called Thax. Peter is still in his cabin in bed. He is still very sick. You go to see him every fifteen minutes. You tell the rest of the crew not to go into Peter's cabin because you do not want them to become sick too.

When you go in to see Peter he says, 'I saw a very big red-and-yellow fly in my cabin. It was about 50 centimetres long. It had one round green eye and it bit me.'

You think Peter was dreaming because it is impossible for a fly like that to hide in the cabin: you could see it too easily. Peter begins to speak again; 'The fly bites humans. It must do this to live. It gets its energy from us.'

You land on Thax. All of you get into the spacecar. This is a little car in the *Colomba*. You can drive around the planet in it. You spray some special chemicals into the *Colomba*. These chemicals will kill all insects in one hour. Do you wait in the spacecar near the *Colomba* (turn to **11**) or do you go round Thax and explore (turn to **60**)?

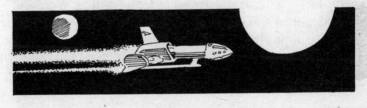

5

You fly around Nirius. Everything seems to be all right. There are no more Platon Warships. You have done a good job. Now you can land on Nirius. Turn to **69**.

6

In the Warship you go to the nearest space station. You think this is a very good idea. You can relax a little bit, check all the equipment and read all the information there. Then you can make your final decision.

When you are about fifteen minutes from the space station, you notice a Platon Warship on the monitor. The Platons are waiting to attack you. You get ready to fight. The Platon Warship fires a missile at you. You immediately fire at them. Your missiles are much quicker and you hit them and destroy their Warship. Their missile does not hit you.

When you arrive at the space station you find that the Platons have destroyed a lot of things. You will need about ten hours to repair everything. Do you stay to repair the space station (turn to **9**) or do you continue to Nirius (turn to **27**)?

7

You think you are safe. After about five minutes, you see five black spots on the monitor again. The Platon Warships quickly come towards you. They are very near. You cannot use your radar-blocking device because they are too near. You try to fire missiles

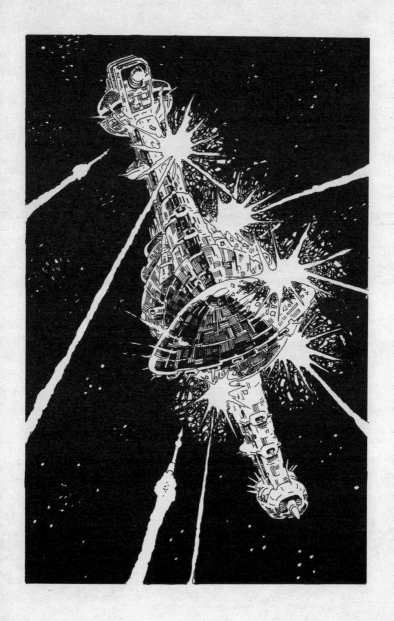

from the right side but you are in the wrong position. It is difficult to hit the Platons like this.

The Platons begin to fire at you. First one Platon ship fires, then another and another. You are hit three times. Your ship is going out of control. You are receiving direct hit after direct hit. Finally your Warship explodes! This is the end of the adventure for you. You are dead. ■

8

Only you and the engineer know about the problem. You tell the engineer to say nothing about the broken energy system. You will watch all of them, your assistant, the two young men, even the engineer, carefully.

You think one of the young men is the enemy. They are new and you have never travelled with them before. But why?

You watch everyone for twenty-four hours. You do not sleep. You are very tired. You soon realize that it is impossible to go on like this. You must sleep. Perhaps the engineer can help you. But are you sure that he is not the enemy? Do you ask the engineer to help you (turn to **12**) or do you try to find the enemy yourself (turn to **20**)?

9

You stay at the space station and begin to repair the equipment. After about half an hour you all begin to feel very tired and sleepy. It is difficult to keep your eyes open. Everyone feels the same. You have a terrible headache, and it is impossible to think.

You are sure this is not an ordinary sickness. You can smell something strange in the air. Suddenly you realize what has happened. When the Platons were here they did something terrible. They put poison into the air system. You cannot breathe. Your engineer falls to the ground. You are very weak and cannot move. Another crew member falls down. The Platons have won. You are dead. They kill you all. This is the end of your adventure. ∎

10

In the Warship you decide to talk to the Nirians. When you switch on the monitor you cannot contact anyone. Your communications system does not work. You realize the Platons are blocking your system. Your equipment is all right because you checked it before you left.

On the Warship you have a second special communications system. You can use it in a situation like this so you can talk to the Nirians. You tell them you are coming to help them. But the Nirians cannot talk to you because their equipment is blocked. They cannot send you any more information.

The Platons have a space station near by. You are now outside Earth's territory. Do you go there to attack them (turn to **33**) or do you go directly to Nirius (turn to **13**)?

11

You wait near the *Colomba*. Peter seems to be a bit better. After about half an hour you hear *Colomba's* engines. Someone has switched them on! How is this possible? You run towards the *Colomba*. A large red-and-yellow head appears at the door of the *Colomba*. A giant fly is standing there. The fly says, 'Now we have your spaceship. We can travel through the Universe. You could not find us on your ship before because we can disappear. Nobody can see us. You must stay on Thax and die. At night there is no oxygen; you cannot breathe.'

You begin to run back to Peter and the others to get your gun. It is too late. The door of the *Colomba* is already shut and it is taking off. There is nothing you can do. You must stay here and die. This is the end of your adventure. You are dead. ■

12

The engineer is alone in the engine room. This is a good time to ask him to help you. 'Mike,' you say, 'Are you absolutely sure that someone has done this terrible thing? Perhaps there's a computer fault?'

'No, Captain,' he says, 'look at this.' He shows you the broken equipment.

'Mike, only you and I have the special identity card that opens the door of the engine room. How could anyone else get in?' you ask.

'Perhaps they copied our cards. Perhaps they stole our cards while we were asleep,' he answers.

'I need your help to find this enemy. I can't do it alone,' you say.

'Yes, I'll help you. We must find the enemy before he does more damage,' says Mike. Turn to **21**.

13

You decide to go directly to Nirius. You switch on the monitor to check your route and present position. You have two possible routes. The first route is very direct but you must pass many Platon space stations. You know they have Warships at these stations and that they will attack you.

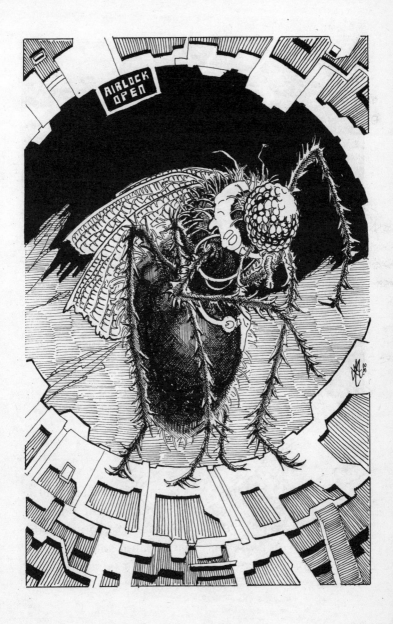

The second route is longer, but there are no problems until you are very close to Nirius. There is a very dangerous area there called 'The Black Hole Triangle'. Many spaceships have disappeared through the Black Hole. Which route do you take? Do you take the first route (turn to **19**) or do you take the second route (turn to **22**)?

14

You go straight back to the *Colomba*. Your job is to help the Nirians. You cannot spend all this time on other problems. You will have to fight the Platons soon, because you are near Nirius. The *Colomba* is ready to continue to Nirius. Turn to **70**

15

You fly the *Colomba* towards the space station. No one lives at the space station. It only collects information for you, or you go there when you have a problem with your spaceship.

You cannot understand what is wrong with your equipment in the *Colomba*. You can talk to Earth but no other planet. Finally you arrive at the space station. You land and get out of the *Colomba*. You

feel good at the space station because you can relax
for a short time. It is more comfortable than in the
Colomba.

Your most important job is to check your equipment. You connect the *Colomba* to the computer-
checking machine. Soon the computer tells you that
there is nothing wrong with your equipment. An
enemy is blocking all contact with other planets. You
believe that the Platons are your enemy. They know
you are trying to help the Nirians. This is very
dangerous. Do you continue in the *Colomba* (turn to
61) or do you ask Earth to send another Warship to
fight the Platons (turn to **43**)?

16

Through the white cotton you see a very big black
spider. It is as big as your spaceship. It begins to
wrap its long hairy legs around the spaceship. You
can do nothing. Your missiles are no good because
the spider is too close. You feel like a fly caught in
a spider's web.

Suddenly, you hear a terrible sound. The spider is
crushing the spaceship. Everything in the control
room is falling to the floor. The spider is pushing the
walls in. You and your crew are crushed to death! I
am sorry, this is the end of your adventure. You are
dead. ■

17

You are very happy that you are in the *Colomba*. It is a slow spaceship and it does not have many special weapons, but you feel safe. You know that other spaceships or Warships will not attack you in the *Colomba*. The Platons will think you are doing routine checks on the space stations. They will not think you are going to help the Nirians. Do you tell the Nirians you are coming (turn to **32**) or do you say nothing so that the Platons will not know what you are doing (turn to **44**)?

18

You want to talk to the young men. You go to their cabin. You have the special computer number to open the door. You do not want to believe there is an enemy on board your ship. You hope this is a mistake and that someone will have a logical explanation.

You go into the young men's cabin. They say, 'Good, now the door is open, we can go to work.'

You stop them and do not let them leave the cabin. 'Wait a moment,' you say, 'I must explain something to you. I believe someone has broken our engines. We have only 50 per cent normal power. Someone on the ship has done this. We have an enemy on board.'

The young men look at you in horror. 'You don't think it is us, do you?' they ask.

'I must ask everyone a lot of questions before I can say anything to anybody. I will bring the lie detector and ask you some questions,' you answer. The lie detector is a machine that shows if someone is telling the truth or lies. Turn to **80**.

19

You continue on the direct route to Nirius. You are in a very dangerous situation now. The Platons at the last space station saw you in the Warship. They will contact all other Platon space stations and tell them.

When you are near the next Platon space station, you see two Platon Warships in front of you. You prepare to fire your missiles. You think the only way to get past them is to kill them.

Your missiles are ready. You fire two of them. The Platons are ready for this and they very quickly change their positions. You miss them. This really surprises you. They fire back at you, but their weapons are not as good as yours and they miss you.

You do not want to use too many of your missiles now because you know that the journey in front of you is long. You fire at the Platons again and use two more missiles. The Platons quickly move, and you miss again. Incredible! These are new Platon

Warships. You have never seen them before. This is a big problem; you are not prepared for this. You continue to Nirius. The Platon Warships are following. Turn to **23**.

20

You will try to find the enemy yourself. You switch on all the monitors. They show you all the rooms in the ship at the same time. It will take a lot of time to watch them. You must also do your other jobs.

You are still worried about the Nirians too, but the problem on the Warship is the most important now. You contact Earth and ask them to send all the information that they have about everyone on the Warship. When will you have time to do all these things? How will you keep things secret from the others?

This evening you are still working. You have not had any sleep. You realize it is impossible to solve the problem like this. You decide to ask the engineer for help after all. Turn to **12**.

21

You begin to walk around the spaceship with the engineer. You watch everyone while they are working. Everything seems quiet. You begin talking to the doctor. Suddenly, there is a terrible explosion. The Warship stops. 'What's happening?' you ask the engineer.

'I don't know, but that explosion came from the engine room. It is the enemy. They have struck again,' he says. Just then, there is another explosion and the whole Warship blows up. This is the end of the adventure for you. You are dead. ■

22

You can go quickly on this second route, but it is long. After about one hour you begin to have problems with the Warship. The Warship is going slower and slower. Something is wrong with the energy; you have no power. When the engineer goes to check this he says, 'Someone has broken the energy system. We

have only half power and it's getting worse. Someone on this ship has done this. There is an enemy among us. Who is it?'

You begin to think. There are only five people on this ship: you, your assistant, the engineer and the two new young men. Why would any of them want to stop you? Could it be one of the young men? They are in their cabin and they do not know what the engineer said.

What are you going to do? You begin to think one of these young men is the enemy but you are not sure ... Do you lock them in their room (turn to **28**) or do you continue and say nothing for the moment (turn to **8**)?

23

You are very angry with yourself because you have fired four missiles without any results. You are also very worried because you see the Platons have new Warships.

You look at the monitor. The two Platon Warships are still following you. You suddenly remember that you have a new piece of equipment on your Warship – a radar-blocking device. When you use this, other Warships cannot see you on their monitors.

You switch it on immediately. After a few minutes, you can see on the monitor that the Platon Warships are not following you any more. They are moving in the wrong direction. This time you are lucky. Turn to **7**.

24

You tell all your crew to get ready for action. You prepare your weapons. Soon everything is ready. You can fire two missiles at the same time. You fire. One Platon Warship explodes immediately. A direct hit! You hit the second one on the side. This Platon Warship fires a missile at you. It hits you on one side. You fire a third missile. This hits the same Platon

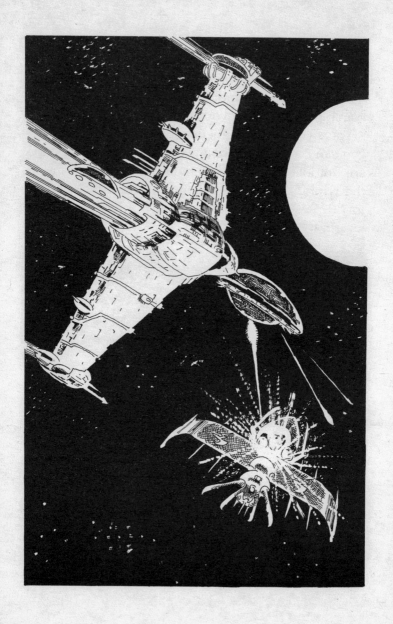

Warship again. This time it is a direct hit! The Platon Warship explodes. The damage to your Warship is not too bad. Do you land on Nirius now (turn to **69**) or do you fly around Nirius to see if there are any other Platon Warships (turn to **5**)?

25

You are in Earth's best Warship. It has many special weapons and can travel very fast. You are with four other people. Two of them are very young and it is their first trip in the Warship.

You are very worried about the Nirians. They are in serious danger. You want to contact the Nirians to tell them you are coming, but the Platons will receive this message too. This will be very dangerous for you. Do you send a message to the Nirians (turn to **10**) or do you say nothing (turn to **54**)?

26

When you wake up, you and the others are on beds connected to the machines. You feel very tired and weak. Then you see the horrible thing next to you. It has a large white head and a small white body. It looks like jelly; you can see through it. It says, 'We have caught you in our trap. You came to help this Earthship, but we sent the S O S message.'

'What are you doing to us and why?' you ask.

'We need your energy to live. We take it with these machines,' it replies.

You know that you will die. Suddenly, you remember you have a mini laser gun in your pocket. If you can get it out and fire it at this creature, you will be free. You are so tired it is difficult to move. Slowly your fingers go to your pocket. The creature is looking at the machine. You feel the gun. You fire it with your last bit of strength. The creature falls to the floor, dead. You free the crew from the other beds. Do you go straight back to the *Colomba* (turn to **14**) or do you go back to the captain on the bed (turn to **31**)?

27

You continue to Nirius. You are coming near to the planet Zor. The Zorians are a very strange people. Their planet is very cold and the people are like ice, but they are very beautiful. They have no feelings, no emotions. They are never happy or sad.

You contact the Ice Queen of Zor and ask if you can pass through her territory. She says, 'Earthmen, I want to talk to you. I will come out in my Warship to meet you. Please wait for me.'

This is very unusual. Normally the Zorians have little contact with any other people. They usually only say yes or no to every question. You wait for the Ice Queen of Zor. Turn to **39**.

28

While the two young men are sleeping in their cabin you lock their door. The lock is automatic. It is controlled by the central computer. It is a really horrible feeling to know that someone on the Warship is an enemy. After about one hour, you begin to think, 'Perhaps it is the engineer, he knows everything about the engines. Perhaps it is my assistant, she knows everything about the Warship.' You begin to worry.

When the two young men wake up they find their door is locked. They cannot understand why. They phone you from their cabin; 'Captain, our door is locked. We do not know what is wrong with it. Please open it for us. We must begin work now.'

You answer, 'I'm sorry, we have some very serious problems. You must stay in your cabin.'

'What do you mean? What problems? Where are the others? What's happening? Please explain,' they reply. Do you go to their cabin and explain (turn to **18**) or do you leave them in their cabin (turn to **76**)?

29

You continue your journey to Nirius. You can talk to Earth but you cannot talk to any other planet. Everything is very quiet. You do not see any other spaceships around you. This is very strange. Suddenly, on your monitor, you see something very large in front of you. You cannot understand what it is. You get a close-up picture on the monitor and you see it is a very old spaceship from Earth. What is it doing here? Perhaps it got lost many years ago. You begin to get a signal from this old spaceship. 'S O S. This is spaceship X25. Please help us. We have no power. We cannot move. S O S.'

This is a very serious situation. You want to continue to Nirius, but what about the X25? Do you decide to stop, and go to help the X25 (turn to **36**) or do you continue directly to Nirius (turn to **50**)?

30

You say to the Queen of Zor, 'I am very sorry but I can't come to Zor now. We're going to Nirius. The Platons are attacking them. We must go to help them.'

The Queen of Zor replies, 'Oh yes, the Platons. I'm sure they will come to Zor too. You're a very brave man. You must fight these terrible people. I hope one day you will come back to us.'

'I hope so too,' you reply. 'But now we must go. It was nice to meet you. Goodbye, Queen of Zor.' You think you see sadness in her eyes as she turns and leaves your spaceship. Turn to **81**.

31

You and the others go back to the captain. You are very tired and it is difficult to walk. The captain is on his bed, and the machine is switched off. You try to wake him up. 'Captain, Captain, wake up. We are taking you on to the *Colomba* with us,' you say.

His eyes begin to open slowly. He tries to speak but he cannot. You and your crew slowly pick him up and carry him towards the door. When you get to the door it opens, and there is another terrible creature standing there.

'You are too late. We are all around this spaceship now,' says the creature. As it speaks a bright light begins to shine. You feel very tired. The captain's body falls out of your hands. You go to sleep. You are the creature's prisoner. You must give your life and energy to these creatures until you die. This is the end of the adventure for you. ■

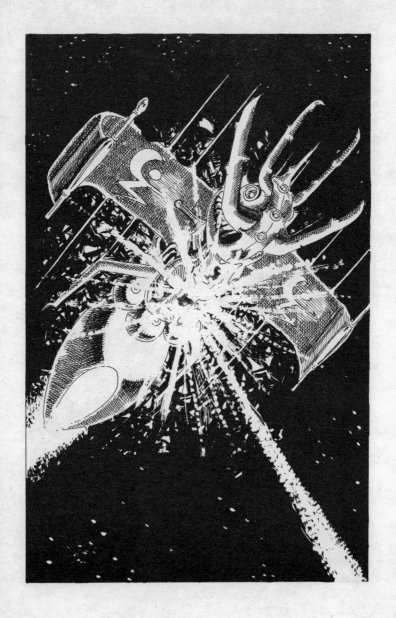

32

You decide to send a computer message to the Nirians. You will not use the monitor to send it because the Platons will see it too. The message will say only that you are coming to visit them and will not mention the problem with the Platons. The Platons will probably check to see what you are doing. When they see you in the *Colomba* they will not attack you. They will believe your message.

You try to send the message to Nirius but something goes wrong and you cannot. Are the Platons already on Nirius or is something wrong with your equipment? Do you go to one of the space stations to check the equipment (turn to **15**) or do you continue your journey to Nirius anyway (turn to **29**)?

33

You decide to go to the Platon station. You must be very careful. The Platons know what you are doing. You switch on your monitor and check the position of the Platon space station. Everything looks good. There are no Platon Warships around you. You must attack this Platon station because they will kill you if they can.

You prepare your missiles. When you fire these missiles they will completely destroy the Platon station. These missiles are fast, accurate and very powerful. You prepare to fire them. You can see that the two young crew members are afraid but excited. You fire your missiles. You hit the Platon station and destroy it. Well done! You continue to Nirius. Turn to **40**.

34

You continue in the Warship towards Nirius. You want to get there as soon as possible. Now you are passing through an area that belongs to the Tan people. They are very clever people. They were very primitive until recently. During the last twenty years they have learnt many things. Nobody really knows very much about them. They have never attacked another planet. You think they are a friendly people.

Suddenly about twenty strange-looking spaceships are all around you. On the monitor T'Oni, the head of the Tans, appears. He says, 'You are passing through our territory and you did not ask for our permission. Why?'

You say, 'We are going to help the Nirians. The Platons have attacked them. I am sorry we did not ask for your permission. I did not know it was necessary.'

T'Oni says, 'You must pay if you want to pass. You must pay not with money but with information. You

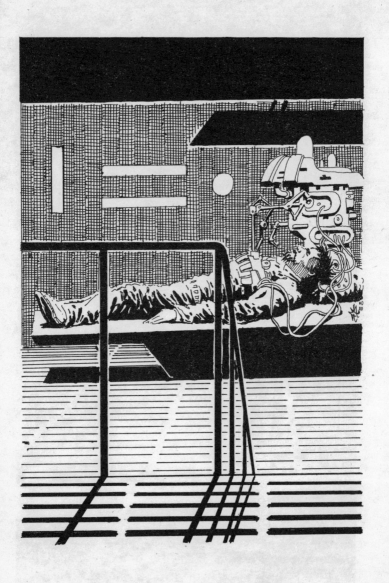

must let us come into your Warship and learn about its new weapons and its secrets. If you do not give us this information, we will attack you and we will always be your enemy.' Do you let T'Oni come into your Warship (turn to **63**) or do you try to pass his Warships without stopping (turn to **38**)?

35

The Platons are near Nirion, the capital of Nirius. You decide to go to the other side of the planet and land there. Just before you land, a Platon Warship appears in front of you. Before you know what is happening, a Platon missile hits the side of your ship. It is too late to land now. The Platons know you are here. Quickly you prepare your missiles and fire at the Platon Warship. You hit it; it is destroyed. You see another two Platon Warships; you fire and you hit them. The last two Platon Warships do not come near you. They go back to Platon. You land on Nirius. Turn to **69**.

36

You go towards the X25. All the time you hear the same S O S message, 'Help us'. You can now see the

X25 more clearly on the monitor. You cannot see any people or any movement. The X25 is hanging in space like a ghost. You stop beside the X25.

You and two others go on to it. When you enter you see a man, the captain, on a bed. At first he looks dead. Then you see he is connected to a big machine. When you look more closely at him, he looks frozen. This spaceship is about four hundred years old. Perhaps the captain froze himself a long time ago when he was in danger. You think you can bring him back to life if you switch on the machine.

Next to the captain there is a cassette machine, and the S O S message is playing all the time. There is something strange about this spaceship and the captain, but you do not know exactly what it is. Do you wake up the captain now (turn to **65**) or do you look round the X25 first (turn to **45**)?

37

You decide to leave Simon and Charles in their cabin with the door locked. You ask the engineer to come to you. 'Hello, Mike, have you looked at the broken equipment? How bad is it?' you ask.

'It's quite bad,' he answers. 'We have enough power to get back to Earth but we haven't got enough to go to Nirius and fight the Platons. That is too dangerous. We must go back to Earth. There is nothing else we can do. I cannot repair the equipment; we need new parts.'

You are very disappointed and angry. This is the end of the adventure for you. You must go back to Earth. ■

38

You cannot show T'Oni your Warship. It is very new and has many secrets. You contact T'Oni and say, 'We cannot stop now. We must go to Nirius to help them. We must pass. Do not try to stop us.'

T'Oni replies, 'You are now our enemy. Be careful!'

Suddenly, without warning, the Tans fire at you. Their weapons are not very good. You go faster and their weapons do not hit you. You quickly leave the Tan area. You have made a new enemy. Turn to **42**.

39

After fifteen minutes you see a large silver spaceship next to your spaceship. You contact the Zorian ship and say, 'The door is open. Come in. Welcome to our ship.'

You wait for the Ice Queen to come from her ship to yours. The automatic doors open. Here is the Ice Queen, standing in front of you. She is the most beautiful woman you have ever seen. She has long blond hair and eyes as blue as the sea. She looks perfect, but she does not smile.

She says, 'I know you are a good person, you are honest, brave and kind. I have heard many good things about you. I want you to come and live on Zor with us and teach us to be happy, to enjoy life. We have everything we need: good food, comfortable houses; but we do not know how to laugh. We have chosen you to teach us. Please come and visit our planet now, and we can talk some more.' Do you go with the Ice Queen to Zor (turn to **72**) or do you say you cannot help her (turn to **30**)?

40

At the moment everything is fine, but the Platons will soon know that you destroyed their space station. You must always watch the monitor to see if any Platon Warships are near you.

After about twenty minutes you suddenly feel the Warship move violently. You think something has hit you. It is very strange because you did not see any Platon Warships on the monitor. The crash was on the left side of the ship. You speak to the engineer, and he goes to see what has happened. When he comes back he says, 'A big ball of ice hit the side of the ship. This is not very dangerous now, but it means we cannot fire our missiles from that side.' Do you continue with the left side of the ship damaged (turn to **59**) or do you stop and repair it (turn to **67**)?

41

You ask the captain again, 'Who are you? Where do you come from?'

The captain says, 'I will answer all your questions later. First press the green button. We must hurry.'

You are not satisfied with this answer, so you ask, 'What are you doing here?'

The captain begins to tell you. 'I came here, just like you, to help this ship. When I came into the ship, there was a very bright light and I couldn't move. Later I found myself on this bed, connected to these machines. They take all the energy from humans. They need it for themselves.'

'Who? Who is doing this to you?' you ask. Just at that moment the machine begins to make a strange noise, and the captain goes into a deep sleep again. Do you try to wake him up (turn to **78**) or do you switch off the machine (turn to **75**)?

42

You continue to Nirius. You can see several Platon Warships on the monitor. They are following you. The Platons will attack you before you get to Nirius. You prepare all your weapons. Your Warship is much better than the Platons' Warships. The problem is that you have only one Warship and they have several. Do you fire at these Platon Warships now (turn to **24**) or do you wait and see what happens (turn to **58**)?

43

You decide to ask Earth for another Warship to help you. Earth tells you that you must wait thirty-six hours. They must check the Warship before they can send it to you. You wait.

At first everything is fine but you are worried about the Nirians. Suddenly the red alarm button on the controls begins to flash, and a warning siren starts.

What is happening? You check the monitors and you
see there are ten Platon Warships around you. Your
weapons are not good enough or fast enough to
attack ten Warships. The ugly green face of the Beast,
King of the Platons, appears on your monitor. He
says, 'I have come to kill you. I will be King of all the
Universe. Earth cannot stop me.' Platon's Warships
fire their missiles. You are dead. This is the end of
your adventure. ■

44

You do not talk to the Nirians because it is too
dangerous. If the Platons know you are helping the
Nirians, they will attack you. You continue your
journey in *Colomba*. After a few hours you realize
there is a problem with the communications system.
You cannot talk to Earth or any other planet. You ask
the engineer, 'What's happening? Is it serious?'

He says, 'The problem is very serious. We must go
to one of our space stations immediately.' Now you
cannot contact anyone. You go to the nearest space
station. Turn to **47**.

45

You suddenly realize what is wrong. The message said, 'We have no power', but, in fact, the 'frozen' captain is connected to a machine, and this machine is switched on. Where is the power coming from?

You leave the main control room with the two other men. Then you go into the engine room where the power comes from. Everything here is silent and black.

Then Mark says, 'I can see some light coming from over there. There is another engine room.' You open the heavy round door. The brightest light you have ever seen hits you in the eyes. There is also a strange sound. The light and the sound paralyse you. You cannot move. Turn to **74**.

46

After about fifteen minutes Captain Jeffreys says he is feeling tired. He goes to his cabin. Now you concentrate on Nirius and the problem there. While you are talking to your crew all the instruments stop. Captain Jeffreys walks into the room with a laser gun in his hand.

'What's happening?' you ask.

'I am a Platon. I have taken control of your ship.

All of you go into the ship's prison,' Captain Jeffreys says. There is nothing you can do. Why did you trust him?

Captain Jeffreys locks all of you in the prison. Soon, a Platon Warship arrives, stops, and several Platons come on to your ship. Turn to **73**.

47

You go in the direction of the nearest space station. You are very afraid because you cannot talk to anyone. You have no contact with Earth.

Suddenly the *Colomba* turns. You cannot control the direction of your spaceship. Something is pulling you in a different direction. You look at your monitor to get some information and you see the ugly green face of the Beast, the King of the Platons. He laughs at you and says, 'You are very stupid, Earthpeople. We know what you are doing. You cannot save the Nirians. In the *Colomba* you can do nothing; you cannot fight us, and of course we must kill you – goodbye.' This is the end of your adventure; you are dead! ■

48

When you are in the middle of the storm everything outside the *Colomba* goes black. You have never seen a storm like this before. Suddenly you realize what is happening. You are coming to a Black Hole. (All space travellers fear Black Holes. Everything that goes near a Black Hole is pulled into it and disappears.) This is why the *Colomba*'s engines cannot move the ship. You try to switch on the emergency power, but this does not help. The Black Hole is beginning to suck the *Colomba* through it. There is nothing you can do. You go through the Black Hole. Turn to **68**.

49

In the old Earth spaceship you go back to the captain. He is still on his bed, and the machine is switched off. You try to wake him up again. 'Captain, Captain, wake up! Speak to us! Tell us what happened!' you shout.

You do not notice that the strange spaceship has come back and is outside. You do not notice the strange creature standing at the door. Then you hear a voice: 'Earthmen.' You look towards the door and see a terrible white creature. It has a huge white head and a very small body. It looks horrible. 'Now

we have caught you. Why did you come back? You are very stupid. We need your energy to live, just like we need the captain's,' the creature says.

The creature has power over you. You cannot understand what it is. You cannot move. The creature takes you and the others and puts you on the beds. Then he connects you to the machines. You go into a long, deep sleep, and the creature takes your energy from you. This is the end of the adventure for you. You stay here until you die! ■

50

You continue in the *Colomba* to Nirius. Peter, the youngest man, says he is feeling sick. His temperature is very high and his arms and legs are shaking. When you examine him in his cabin you find a small but very strange insect bite on his arm. You take some blood from him and put it in the medical analyser. This machine can immediately identify any sickness.

After a few minutes the machine says that this is a completely new sickness; it is very dangerous and it comes from an insect. Is a strange insect living on *Colomba*? You must land immediately on the nearest planet. You must find the insect and kill it. Peter is now very sick. He cannot talk or move. You decide to land on the nearest planet.

Turn to **4**.

51

You think the young men, Simon and Charles, are not the enemy. You decide to give them another chance. You speak to them on the internal phone and say, 'OK, we have solved the problem; you can open your door and go to work now.'

After about thirty minutes there is a terrible explosion. It is in the engine room. All the alarms start ringing. All the engines stop. Simon and Charles run into the control room. 'What's happening?' you ask.

'We have blown up the engine room. You cannot continue to Nirius. The Platons paid us a lot of money to do this before we left Earth. The Platons

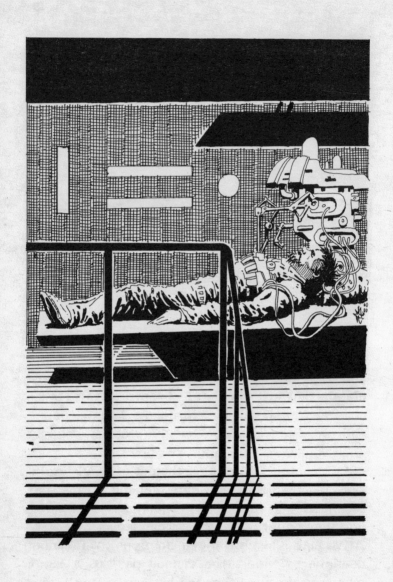

will come in a minute and take us back with them. Then they will blow up this Warship,' Charles says. This is the end of the adventure for you. You are dead. ■

52

You switch on the monitor and tell Earth that you want another Warship to help you. Earth replies, 'We cannot send you another Warship at the moment. You know we do not have many Warships because we are a peaceful people. Our other Warships are at the other end of the Universe where there is a lot of trouble. You must continue alone.' Turn to **42**.

53

You say to T'Oni, 'All right, I'll show you our Warship.' You begin to show him around your Warship. He looks at the central controls, the weapons and all the special equipment. T'Oni is very interested and asks many questions. All the time his two gunmen follow you. You feel very uncomfortable. Then you say to T'Oni, 'This is all I can show you now. We are in a hurry. We must go and fight the Platons. This is the best way we can help you.'

'T'Oni laughs and says to his men, 'Take him!' They hold you and point their guns at you. T'Oni says to your men, 'If anyone tries to help him, we will kill your captain. Now we are going to take your Warship, and you are going to be our prisoners on Tan.' You must go with T'Oni as his prisoner. You must live on Tan and you can never escape. This is the end of the adventure for you. ■

54

You do not talk to the Nirians. You want to surprise the Platons. If you stay silent, the Platons will not know you are going to Nirius. You and the four other people on *Colomba* check all the equipment. You are sure you can help the Nirians. You decide to go there as quickly as possible.

Soon you are leaving the boundaries of Earth's empire. There is a space station here, just beyond the boundary. It collects information about everything that is happening. Do you go to this space station because you want to know the exact position and number of the Platon Warships (turn to **6**) or do you continue directly to Nirius (turn to **57**)?

55

You walk around for about forty-five minutes. This place makes you feel very relaxed. It is very beautiful. You would like to stay here, but you know you must go to Nirius. You go back to your spaceship with the others and take off again. You are very pleased that you have seen this planet. Turn to **70**.

56

You continue to Nirius. You are now going through a new area. Nobody has ever been here before. You have passed the storm, so there is no danger now. However, you are worried about taking a long time to get to Nirius. Perhaps the Platons have killed the Nirians; perhaps you are too late. While you are thinking about this something white, like cotton, appears on the monitor. What is it? You look at the other monitors. They show you different parts of the *Colomba* outside. You can see this white thing everywhere, covering the *Colomba*. All the time it is getting thicker and thicker. It looks like a giant spider's web. Turn to **16**.

57

You decide to go quickly to Nirius. It is very important to check your route and the positions of the Platon Warships. You switch on the monitor to get this information from the space station. No information comes through. When you look at the space station on the monitor you can see someone has attacked it. Many parts of the station are destroyed and the equipment is broken.

Suddenly the picture on the monitor changes. You see the ugly green face of the Beast, King of the Platons. He laughs at you and says, 'Ha, ha, Earth-people. Do you think you can help the Nirians? We will kill you before you get there. You see we have destroyed your space station here. We will destroy you. Go back before we kill you.' Then the face disappears from the monitor. Do you continue to Nirius (turn to **34**) or do you think the situation is too dangerous? Perhaps you should wait and ask Earth to send another Warship to help you (turn to **52**).

58

You speak to the engineer and ask him, 'Have the Platons already attacked Nirius, or are they waiting to attack?'

'They have already attacked because we can see red balls of fire on Nirius. These are the spots where they have fired their missiles and hit something.' Now you know this you get ready to attack the Platon Warships. Turn to **24**.

59

You continue to Nirius. You hope that no one attacks you because you can only fire missiles from the right side of the Warship.

After about half an hour you see five black spots on the monitor. They are a long way away. Every minute they are getting closer. After five minutes you are sure: they are Platon Warships. Now you wish you had stopped and repaired your Warship.

You suddenly remember that this new Warship has a radar-blocking device. You have never used this equipment before. Other enemy spaceships cannot see you on their radar when you use it. They cannot fire missiles at you. You switch on your radar-blocking device. The Platon Warships cannot see you and they start moving in strange directions. After a while they go away. You are very lucky this time but, remember, the Platons will come back! Turn to **7**.

60

You land on Thax. When you go over a hill you find a town. Everything is empty and broken down. You begin to look at the houses and other buildings. There are no people, only very old things: a type of car, furniture and machines. You realize there has been a war here. A long time ago a bomb – like a nuclear bomb or, perhaps, a chemical bomb – exploded here. All living things are dead. You feel very sad and wonder why there is always war some- where in the Universe. You go back to the *Colomba* after one hour. Peter is a little better. You take off again and continue to Nirius. Turn to **70**.

61

You leave the space station in the *Colomba*. You cannot talk to the Nirians from your spaceship so you want to go to Nirius as quickly as possible. After about thirty minutes you see, on the monitor, a meteor storm in front of you. The *Colomba* is old and

not very strong. If you go through the storm, it will damage the *Colomba*. Then you will be in serious trouble. If you go round the storm and change your route, you will lose ten hours. Do you go through the storm (turn to **66**) or do you go round the storm and lose ten hours (turn to **3**)?

62

You say to T'Oni, 'We cannot help you now because we must go to Nirius. The Platons are attacking them.'

T'Oni says, 'You will not help us? Then you are our enemy.' He looks at his two gunmen and shouts, 'Fire!' You cannot believe what is happening. Your men try to get their guns, but you were not prepared for this. In a couple of minutes T'Oni has killed all of you and has taken your Warship. This is the end of the adventure for you. You are dead! ■

63

You decide to let T'Oni come on to your Warship. You hope you can explain the situation to him. You do not want him to become your enemy, but you do not want to show him all the secrets of your Warship.

You say, 'Come to our Warship, T'Oni, and we can talk together.'

'I will come immediately,' T'Oni replies.

Soon T'Oni arrives. You watch him on the monitor. He leaves his spaceship. He is not alone; he is with two other men. When T'Oni comes into the cabin, the two other men are holding guns. You do not like this and you say to him, 'Do you come as our friend or our enemy? Why have your men got their guns? This isn't necessary.'

T'Oni says, 'We must learn about your weapons. The Platons are attacking Nirius. After Nirius they will attack us. They will come to Tan. We must protect ourselves.' This is a very difficult decision for you. Do you believe T'Oni and show him your weapons (turn to 53) or do you say you will not help him (turn to 62)?

64

Captain Jeffreys sends a message to his friend on Platon. He sends it in a secret code so that no one can understand it. He explains the situation and asks for information about Nirius. Soon a message comes back. The friend says that six Platon Warships are going to the capital, Nirion, with their missiles ready to fire. With your long-distance radar you find the Platon Warships. You can prepare your missiles.

You fire and hit four Platon Warships. They are destroyed. You immediately fire another two missiles and hit the last two Platon Warships. Well done. You have killed all the Platons in their Warships. Now you can land on Nirius. Turn to **69**.

65

You look very carefully at all the controls on the machine. You are sure you can operate it. The machine is on, a red light is flashing and you can see some movement in the captain's body. You watch him closely. You still think there is something strange about this man. Slowly his eyes open. When you look into his pale blue eyes you feel cold and frightened. Mark and John look at the man, then at you, nervously. 'This man is not human!' says Mark.

Perhaps he is right. When you look again at the captain's eyes you think he is a robot not a human. You cannot understand what he is doing here on this very old Earth spaceship. The captain begins to speak: 'Press the green button on the machine. Then I can get up and walk.'

'Who are you? What are you doing here?' you ask.

'Press the green button; do it now!' the captain shouts. You do not know if the captain is a friend or an enemy. Do you press the green button (turn to **77**) or do you ask the captain more questions (turn to **41**)?

66

You decide to go through the storm in the *Colomba*. You watch the monitor all the time. The storm is getting bigger and bigger and nearer and nearer. You have five minutes before you hit the storm. You switch *Colomba*'s engines to maximum speed and maximum power. All of you sit in your seats and put your seatbelts on. You know there will be a lot of movement when you go through the storm.

Now the storm hits you. The *Colomba* nearly stops, then starts again. Perhaps the engine is not strong enough to get you through the storm. There is a terrible crash; a lot of equipment falls on to the floor. The crash knocks you from side to side. The engine is working, but you are not moving forward. The engine is not strong enough. You hope the storm will pass soon. Turn to **48**.

67

You decide to stop and repair the damaged side of the Warship. You must switch off all your engines to stop. Then the engineer and one other man must go outside in a small spacecar. They must repair the pipe so that the missiles can come out of the pipe. While they are doing this you must also switch off

all the missile controls. If you do not, it is very dangerous.

The engineer and Luke get into the spacecar. You are very worried about them because of the Platons. If they come now, there is nothing you can do to stop them. You begin to count the minutes. You hope everything will be OK. Nobody says anything. Everybody is very nervous. You are watching the engineer and Luke on the monitor.

Suddenly you see two Platon Warships. What can you do? Your engines and missiles are switched off. The Platons fire at the spacecar; Luke and the engineer are killed! Then the Platons fire at you and you are killed. This is the end of the adventure for you! ■

68

There is a terrible noise. The *Colomba* goes through the Black Hole at an incredible speed. You think your head is going to explode. You all look at each other with terrified eyes. Suddenly everything is calm; you are floating in another Universe. All the equipment on the *Colomba* is broken. You know it is impossible to get back through the Black Hole. I am sorry, this is the end of your adventure. You have disappeared in space, like many other spacemen. Goodbye. ■

69

You land on Nirius. In Nirion, the capital, everyone comes out to meet you. You are the heroes. You have saved the Nirians from the most terrible people, the Platons. You contact Earth and tell them that you have succeeded in your mission. The Nirians are free, and the Platons are destroyed!

The Nirians prepare a great party with food, drink, dancing and music. At last you can relax and enjoy yourselves. After a few days you will return to Earth again, as heroes. Well done!

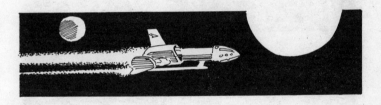

70

You continue to Nirius. You can see the planet Nirius on your monitor now. You can also see six Platon Warships around Nirius. You know this is the moment you have all been waiting for. You must kill the Platons. The Platon Warships begin to fire their missiles at Nirius. They have not seen you. They are too interested in Nirius.

You prepare yourself, the crew and the *Colomba* for the attack. The *Colomba* is old, but it can fire its missiles quite quickly. You fire four missiles. Immediately four of the Platon Warships explode and disappear into the blackness. The other two Platon Warships suddenly realize what is happening. They turn to fire at you. They are too late. You fire at them and destroy them too. They are all dead. You can land on Nirius now. Turn to **69**.

71

You land on the green planet. There is oxygen here so you can breathe fresh air and you can walk without your spacesuits. You get out of the *Colomba* and see a beautiful place. There is perfume in the air. There are trees with lovely flowers and fruit. There is water running into a pool. The climate is wonderful – just the right temperature. You and the others decide to walk further. While you are walking you begin to hear music. You walk in the direction of the music. It is coming from a cave. The others

want to go into the cave. You feel frightened. You think you will never come out again. Do you go into the cave (turn to **79**) or do you walk away (turn to **55**)?

72

You go with the Queen of Zor in her spaceship. Soon you land on the planet Zor. The Queen takes you to her palace. It is the most beautiful place you have ever seen. You cannot believe it is true; it is like a dream. The air is full of perfume and there is music. The Queen of Zor says, 'Please stay with us and teach us all you know.'

You say, 'I'm very sorry we can't stay here now. We are travelling to Nirius to help the Nirians because the Platons are attacking them.'

'Yes, the Platons are a terrible people. They will kill all of us. You are very brave. I understand you must go to help the Nirians. When your mission is finished will you come back here?' the Queen of Zor asks.

'I will return to Earth, if my mission is successful. Then I hope I can come back here to you,' you reply. The Queen gives you something to drink. You feel very relaxed and calm. What a pity you cannot stay here now, but you must go on to Nirius. Turn to **81**.

73

In your Warship you go to Nirius. The Platons prepare the missiles. They are going to attack Nirius, and there is nothing you can do. You cannot stop them.

The Beast, King of the Platons, comes to the prison and says, 'We do not need you any more. We have your Warship; this is what we needed. Now you know the Platons are the greatest people in the Universe and you must die. You are our enemy.' He takes out his laser gun and kills all of you. This is the end of the adventure for you. You are dead. ■

74

You cannot move; you cannot speak; you just stand there. You can still think and see and hear. You look around the room. There are several beds connected to machines. They are exactly the same as the

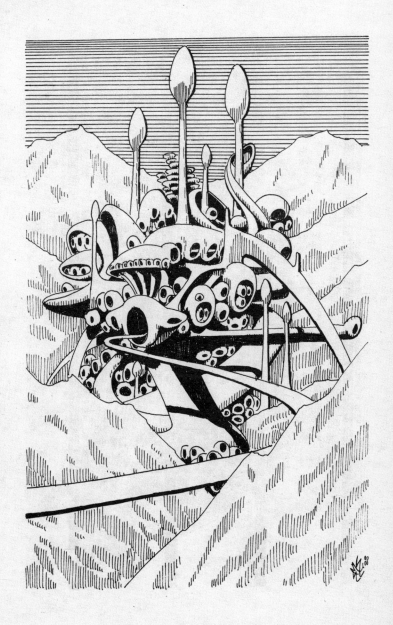

captain's bed. Suddenly, you feel a strange energy enter your body. This energy picks you up and carries you to one of these beds. You have no control over your movements. The same thing is happening to the others. On the bed you go into a deep sleep. Turn to **26**.

75

You quickly switch off the machine. When you touch the captain he is very cold. You say, 'Captain, Captain, wake up.'

His eyes open for a minute and he says, 'They have taken all my energy. I'm dying. You must leave this place quickly, before they come back. Go!' These are his last words. He dies in your arms. You must go now and continue to Nirius. Turn to **70**.

76

You leave the young men in their cabin. You switch on the monitor. You can see and hear them on the monitor. You listen to their conversation. One of the young men is called Simon, the other Charles. If you secretly listen to their conversation, perhaps you can discover if they are the enemy or not.

Simon says, 'I wonder what is happening. Why doesn't the captain explain to us? I hope there isn't a serious problem with the Warship. Perhaps it's only a problem with the automatic door-locking system.' 'I think it's more serious,' says Charles. 'The captain was very strange when he talked to us. Normally he explains everything.' Simon and Charles continue talking in this way. Do you believe they are not the enemy and you have made a mistake (turn to **51**) or do you think they are very clever and they are the enemy (turn to **37**)?

77

You press the green button. The captain begins to move. He slowly sits up, then he carefully puts his feet on the floor. He does not speak or move for a few minutes. You wonder what is going to happen next. The captain is holding his head in his hands. Finally he speaks: 'Thank goodness you helped me. I am Captain Jeffreys.' When you look into his face now, you can see it has changed. He is a human. The captain continues: 'I found this ship and I came aboard to help the people, but I couldn't find anyone. Then there was a very bright light, and I could not move. I went to sleep. When I woke up I was on this bed, connected to this machine. All my energy and intelligence were going into this machine.

I went to sleep again. The next time I woke up I saw a strange figure beside me. It was like a human but with a very big head and a small body. It was white, and I could see through it. It was horrible. I asked this figure, 'What are you doing to me?' and it replied, 'We need your energy to live. We must keep you here.. We need more humans, not only you,' I was terrified. Now we must go quickly before these figures come back. They will take you too.' Turn to **82**.

78

'Captain, Captain, don't go to sleep! You must tell me more!' you shout. You try to shake him, but he is in a deep sleep. You cannot wake him up. At that moment you hear another spaceship. You look out through the window and see a very strange space-ship. You quickly shout to the others, 'Let's go back to the *Colomba*! I'm not sure what is going on, but we will be safer there.'

In the *Colomba* you watch the other spaceship. They see you in the *Colomba* but they circle around the old Earth spaceship. They do not attack you. You try to contact them on your communications system. 'Who are you? What are you doing here?' you ask. There is no answer. After a few minutes the strange spaceship goes away again. Do you continue to Nirius (turn to **70**) or do you go back into the old Earth spaceship (turn to **49**)?

79

When you enter the cave there are lots of flashing lights dancing in the air. A voice says, 'What are you doing here, Earthmen?'

You say, 'We are going to Nirius. Your planet looked very beautiful, and we wanted to see it. We were curious.'

The voice continues, 'Don't you know no one ever leaves the Green Planet? It is dangerous to be curious. We have the secret of life here, and that's why no one can leave. Perhaps you would like to meet the other Earthmen who are on our planet.'

You are amazed. The figures of four Earthmen come out of the lights. They have the bodies of humans, but differently coloured lights are coming out of their eyes. You recognize one of the men. It is Captain Edwards. He left Earth many years ago

and no one ever knew what happened to him. You say, 'Captain Edwards, are you OK? I will take you back to Earth in my spaceship.'

'You cannot,' replies Captain Edwards. 'You will never leave here. They have already taken your ship. You will live here for ever with us. They will give you the secret of life. This is Paradise but prison too. You have no choice.' This is the end of your adventure. You live for ever here on the Green Planet. ■

80

You leave the two young men in their cabin and go back to the central control room. You switch on the monitor to their room. Simon, is saying, 'Be quiet. Don't say anything, perhaps he is listening to us.' Now you are almost sure they are the enemy. You still do not understand why. You get the lie detector and go back to their cabin.

'Do you have the right to do this to us?' Charles asks.

'Yes,' you answer, 'I am the captain. I can do anything to protect my ship.' You switch on the lie detector. At this moment Charles hits you, and you fall to the floor. Simon and Charles cannot get out of the room because only you can open the door. 'That was a stupid thing to do,' you say. 'If you are innocent, why fight me?' They will not answer you.

You press the alarm button and ask the engineer and the doctor to come to the cabin. When they come you explain everything to them. The doctor connects the lie detector to Simon's arm. 'Did you break our energy system?' you ask.

'No,' says Simon. The lie detector shows that he is lying.

'OK, we know you are lying, but why?' you ask.

'All right, I'll tell you why. Before we left Earth the Platons contacted us. They paid us a lot of money to do this,' says Charles. 'We must put you in the prison until we get back to Earth. The engineer says you must go back to Earth now because you have not got enough energy to continue to Nirius.' You are very disappointed. You must return to Earth. This is the end of the adventure for you. ■

81

You continue to Nirius. Soon you are quite near Nirius. You can see several Platon Warships; they are flying very near Nirius. You can also see one or two red balls of fire burning on Nirius. This means the Platons have already attacked Nirius. Do you attack the Platon Warships now (turn to 2) or do you secretly land on Nirius (turn to 35)?

82

You believe what Captain Jeffreys says. You quickly go back to the *Colomba*. When you are on board, Captain Jeffreys says, 'You saved my life, thank you. What are you doing in this part of the Universe? I didn't think anyone would find me.'

'We are going to Nirius to fight the Platons,' you answer.

'I would like to help you,' Captain Jeffreys says. 'I know the Platons well. Many years ago they were a friendly people, but their new King, the Beast, is terrible. The Platon people do not like him. I have a friend on Platon, a very good man. Shall I contact him on your monitor? Perhaps he can help you.' Do you think Captain Jeffreys can help you, and that he should contact his friend on Platon (turn to **64**) or do you think it is better to continue as before (turn to **46**)?

GLOSSARY

adventure an exciting or dangerous situation

attack to try to hurt someone, to fight with someone

beast a large, dangerous, wild animal

bite to use teeth to cut through something

blow up to explode

board; on board on a ship, train or aeroplane

boundaries limits, frontiers

brave (person) someone who has courage, not afraid of danger

breathe take air into the body through the mouth

cave a large hole in the side of a hill or cliff

crew the people who work on a ship, spaceship or aeroplane

creature an animal

crush to press very hard so that you break something

damage to harm something so that it stops working or it is broken

destroy to damage so much that there is nothing left

enemy someone who hates you, someone who is not your friend

equipment the things you use for a job

expert a person who is very good at something, a person who has studied something a lot

explode to burst or blow up loudly

explosion a sudden loud burst from a bomb

fault a mistake, something wrong

galaxy a big group of stars and planets
hurry to do something quickly
lie to say something which is not true
lock to close something with a key
mention to say
noise a sound that you do not like
miss you do not hit something
missile a weapon, something to kill or destroy others
peaceful calm, quiet
receive to get
relax to feel calm and comfortable
routine (trip) a normal or typical trip
sad unhappy
sick ill
solve a problem to find the answer
steal to take something which is not yours
trap where you catch an animal or a person
trust someone to believe someone
ugly not beautiful
weak not strong
weapon something like a gun, knife or missile
worried unhappy because you are thinking about some problems